In God We Trust

WestBow Press books may be ordered through booksellers or by contacting:

WestBow Press
A Division of Thomas Nelson & Zondervan
1663 Liberty Drive
Bloomington, IN 47403
www.westbowpress.com
1 (866) 928-1240

This is a work of fiction. All of the characters, names, incidents, organizations, and dialogue in this novel are either the products of the author's imagination or are used fictitiously.

ISBN: 978-1-9736-3040-1 (sc)
ISBN: 978-1-9736-3885-8 (hc)
ISBN: 978-1-9736-3041-8 (e)

Library of Congress Control Number: 2018906879

Printed in the United States of America.

WestBow Press rev. date: 3/29/2019

WESTBOW
PRESS®
A DIVISION OF THOMAS NELSON
& ZONDERVAN

To
River

Dear Readers,

I would like to share my story about how this book began. Eight years ago, my daughter Nicole was going to college and had a job as a nanny. Eva, the little girl she was caring for loved to sing the "Itsy Bitsy Spider" and constantly asked Nicole to sing it to her multiple times a day. When my daughter told me about Eva, the "Itsy Bitsy Spider" tune began to hum in my head... but the words simply changed. The Spirit led me to call my 70 year old Aunt Syble, and I asked her if she could still sing "Itsy Bitsy Spider." She recited it as eager as Eva, as if she were 4 again. When I hung up the phone, I had a strong feeling the Lord was telling me to teach children to sing His truth when they are young, so that when they are old, they will still remember the Word. So many of the "remixes" in this book have similar personal stories behind them, and I have been amazed at the ways the Lord has led me to scripture that would back up what was just written. I hope this book sparks your childlike faith as you and your little ones travel through the pages.

"I will sing to the Lord because he is good to me."

—Psalm 13:6 (NLT)

Dance

You put your left hip in!
You put your left hip out!
You put your whole self in
And dance all about!
Sing Hallelujah,
Laugh, and tell about—
He delivers, have no doubt!

Hidden Treasure

For everything there is a season, a time for every activity under heaven. ... A time to cry and a time to laugh. A time to grieve and a time to dance.

—Ecclesiastes 3:1, 4 (NLT)

Yes, and the Lord will deliver me from every evil attack and will bring me safely into his heavenly Kingdom. All glory to God forever and ever! Amen.

—2 Timothy 4:18 (NLT)

Clue: Sing to the tune of, "The Hokey Pokey."

Take-a-Stone, Take-a Stone

Take-a-stone, take a stone, chosen son,
watch your giants fall one by one.
Take it and sling it and listen for the sound,
Yes it's your enemies falling to the ground!

Hidden Treasure

Strengthen the man you love, the son of your choice.

—Psalm 80:17 (NLT)

As Goliath moved closer to attack, David quickly ran out to meet him. Reaching into his shepherds bag and taking out a stone, he hurled it with his sling and hit the Philistine in the forehead. The stone sank in, and Goliath stumbled and fell face down on the ground.

—1 Samuel 17:48-49 (NLT)

Clue: Sing to the tune of, "Pat-a-Cake, Pat-a-Cake."

Armor

Helmet,
Breastplate,
Belt, and boots!
Belt and boots!
Sword of the Spirit
and the shield of faith—
Armor on and all in place!
All in place!

Hidden Treasure

A final word: Be strong in the Lord and in his mighty power. Put on all of God's armor so that you will be able to stand firm against all strategies of the devil.

—Ephesians 6:10–11 (NLT)

Clue: Sing to the tune of, "Head, Shoulders, Knees & Toes."

Twinkle, Twinkle, Morning Star

Twinkle, twinkle, Morning Star. On your throne is where you are.
Humbly at your feet I bow.
Intercede for me now.
Twinkle, twinkle, Morning Star. On your throne is where you are.
Fix my eyes on things above,
Trusting in your perfect love.
Twinkle, twinkle, Morning Star. On your throne is where you are.

Hidden Treasure

Who will bring any charge against those whom God has chosen? Who is he that condemns? Christ Jesus, who died—more than that, who was raised to life—is at the right hand of God and is also interceding for us.

—Romans 8:33-34 (NIV)

Set your mind on things above, not on earthly things.

—Colossians 3:2 (NIV)

"I Jesus have sent my angel to give you this testimony for the churches. I am the Root, and the Offspring of David, and the bright and Morning Star."

—Revelation 22:16 (NIV)

Clue: Sing to the tune of, "Twinkle, Twinkle, Little Star."

Little Boy Ben

Little boy Ben,
Come thank the Lord
For the sheep in your meadow,
The cows and fields of corn.
Steward well, little boy,
what He entrusted to you.
Work hard without complaining; be generous and true.
Walk in his ways, and always forgive:
This is the way we have taught you to live.

Hidden Treasure

Train up a child in the way he should go; even when he is old he will not depart from it.
—Proverbs 22:6 (ESV)

My son, keep your father's command and do not forsake your mother's teaching.
—Proverbs 6:20 (NIV)

Whatever you do, work at it with all your heart, as working for the Lord, not for men, since you know you will receive an inheritance from the Lord as a reward. It is the Lord Christ you are serving.
—Colossians 3:23-24 (NIV)"

Clue: Sing to the tune of, "Little Boy Blue."

Will Not Bow

Shadrach, Meshach, and Abednego,
On their knees they would not go.
They left their fate in God's hands
And would not bow at Neb's command.
Mordecai did the same.
Tables turned
And he remained.
"Bow, bow"
Will come again,
But I will trust
And receive no mark from him.
Six-six-six on me, no way!
For I have been taught
To trust and obey!

Hidden Treasure

If we are thrown into the blazing furnace, the God we serve is able to save us from it, and he will rescue us from your hand, O king. But even if he does not, we want you to know, O king, that we will not serve your gods or worship the image of gold you have set up.

—Daniel 3:17–18 (NIV)

All the royal officials at the king's gate knelt down and paid honor to Haman, for the king had commanded this concerning him. But Mordecai would not kneel down or pay him honor.

—Esther 3:2 (NIV)

A third angel followed them and said in a loud voice: "If anyone worships the beast and his image and receives his mark on the forehead or on the right hand, he too will drink of the wine of God's fury, which has been poured full strength into a cup of his wrath. He will be tormented with burning sulfur in the presence of the holy angels and of the Lamb."

—Revelation 14:9–10 (NIV)

Mikey Likey

Mikey likey, milk, and pie,
Keep from the things that make you lie.
If they call for you to play,
Mikey likey, run away!

Hidden Treasure

Do not be deceived: "Bad company ruins good morals."

—1 Corinthians 15:33 (ESV)

Run from anything that stimulates youthful lusts. Instead, pursue righteous living, faithfulness, love, and peace. Enjoy the companionship of those who call upon the Lord with pure hearts.

—2 Timothy 2:22 (NLT)

My son, if sinners entice you, do not consent.

—Proverbs 1:10 (ESV)

Clue: Sing to the tune of, "Georgie Porgie."

An Itsy Bitsy Prayer

An itsy bitsy prayer went up for God to hear.
Down came His love and washed away the fear.
Out came the Son, and took me by the hand.
And my itsy bitsy heart is calmed once again.

Hidden Treasure

Yet I still belong to you; you hold my right hand. You guide me with your counsel, leading me to a glorious destiny. Whom have I in heaven but you? I desire you more than anything on earth.

—Psalm 73:23–25 (NLT)

Clue: Sing to the tune of, "Itsy Bitsy Spider."

Washed from Above

Rub-a-dub-dub, I am washed from above.
Because of His grace I shall get there—
My Father, my Maker,
My sin and shame taker.
They all wash out, like suds from my hair.
A cleansing like that—nothing can compare!

Hidden Treasure

And since we have a great High Priest who rules over God's house, let us go right into the presence of God with sincere hearts fully trusting him. For our guilty consciences have been sprinkled with Christ's blood to make us clean and our bodies have been washed with pure water.

—Hebrews 10:21-22 (NLT)

Clue: Sing to the tune of, "Rub a Dub Dub."

Sing Out Loud

Sing, sing, sing out loud.
Praise His holy name.
Powerfully, powerfully, powerfully
The Lord Almighty reigns.

Clap, clap, clap your hands.
Tell about His fame.
Mightily, mightily, mightily
The Lord Almighty reigns.

Hidden Treasure

For you make me glad by your deeds, O Lord; I sing for joy at the works of your hands.
— Psalm 92:4 (NIV)

Then I heard what sounded like a great multitude, like the roar of rushing waters and like loud peals of thunder, shouting: "Hallelujah! For our Lord God Almighty reigns."
— Revelation 19:6 (NIV)

Clue: Sing to the tune of "Row, Row, Row your Boat."

Old King Saul

Old King Saul was a troubled soul,
and a troubled soul was he.
He called for David so the spirit would take flight,
and the spirit did surely flee!

David did play a handy harp,
and a handy harp he played.
Oh, so rare, from sheep to armor-bearer,
with Old King Saul he stayed.

Hidden Treasure

Whenever the spirit from God came upon Saul, David would take his harp and play. Then relief would come to Saul; he would feel better, and the evil spirit would leave him.

— 1 Samuel 16:23 (NIV)

Clue: Sing to the tune of "Old King Cole."

Knock, Knock

Knock, knock.
Who's there?
God.
God who?
The one who gave His Son for you.
Knock, knock.
Come on in.
It's good to see you, my friend!

Hidden Treasure

For God so loved the world that he gave his one and only Son, that whoever believes in him shall not perish but have eternal life.

— John 3:16 (NIV)

Look! I stand at the door and knock, if you hear my voice and open the door, I will come in, and we will share a meal together as friends.

— Revelation 3:20 (NLT)

Princess, Pull the Plank Out

Princess, pull the plank out.
Princess, pull the plank out.
Princess, pull the plank out
So you may see.
Seeing you can help a friend.
Seeing you can help a friend.
Seeing you can help a friend,
For we all have strayed.

Hidden Treasure

Why do you look at the speck of sawdust in your brother's eye and pay no attention to the plank in your own eye? How can you say to your brother, "Brother, let me take the speck out of your eye," when you yourself fail to see the plank in your own eye? You hypocrite, first take the plank out of your eye, and then you will see clearly to remove the speck from your brother's eye.

— Luke 6:41–42 (NIV)

We all, like sheep, have gone astray, each of us has turned to his own way; and the Lord has laid on him the iniquity of us all.

— Isaiah 53:6 (NIV)

Clue: Sing to the tune of " Polly Put Kettle On."

Molly and Me

Molly, my sister, and I fell out,
And what do you think it was all about?
She loved pleasure, and I loved God,
And that is the reason things went all wrong.
"Molly, don't go down that road!"
She shrugged her shoulders and said, "Leave me alone."

Hidden Treasure

But mark this: There will be terrible times in the last days. People will be lovers of themselves, lovers of money, boastful, proud, abusive, disobedient to their parents, ungrateful, unholy, without love, unforgiving, slanderous, without self-control, brutal, not lovers of the good, treacherous, rash, conceited, lovers of pleasure rather than lovers of God, having a form of godliness but denying its power. Have nothing to do with such people.

—2 Timothy 3:1–5 (NIV)

Clue: Sing to the tune of, "Coffee and Tea."

Are You Praying?

Are you praying?
Are you praying,
Little one, little one?
Father loves to listen. Father loves to listen.
Pray along.
Sing a song.

Hidden Treasure

Always be joyful. Never stop praying. Be thankful in all circumstances, for this is God's will for you who belong to Christ Jesus.

—1 Thessalonians 5:16–18 (NLT)

I love the Lord because he hears my voice and prayer for mercy. Because he bends down to listen, I will pray as long as I have breath!

—Psalm 116:1–2 (NLT)

Clue: Sing to the tune of, "I Hear Thunder."

Do you Know the Son of Man?

Do you know the Son of Man, the Son of Man,
The Son of Man?
Oh, do you know the Son of Man
who lives and reigns?

Oh yes, I know the Son of Man, the Son of Man,
The Son of Man.

Oh yes, I know the Son of Man.
Jesus is His name.

Hidden Treasure

Jesus said, "I Am. And you will see the Son of Man seated in the place of power at God's right hand and coming on the clouds of heaven."

—Mark 14:62 (NLT)

Clue: Sing to the tune of, "Do You Know the Muffin Man."

Hilary, Emery, Brock

Hilary, Emery, Brock,
God watches your clock.
No need to fear;
He's always near.
He is your
Helper, Deliverer, Rock!

Hidden Treasure

My help comes from the Lord, the Maker of heaven and earth ... the Lord will watch over your coming and going both now and forevermore.

—Psalm 121:2, 8 (NIV)

My times are in your hands; deliver me from my enemies, and from those you pursue me.

—Psalm 31:15 (NIV)

For I am the Lord your God, who takes hold of your right hand and says to you, Do not fear; I will help you.

—Isaiah 41:13 (NIV)

Clue: Sing to the tune of, "Hickory, Dickory, Dock."

I See Lightning

I see lightning. I see lightning,
Arrows too, arrows too.
Little heart, fear not.
Little heart, fear not.
I am safe,
Held by You.

Hidden Treasure

There you saw how the LORD your God carried you, as a father carries a son, all the way you went until you reached this place.

—Deuteronomy 1:31 (NLV)

Hurl your lightning bolts and scatter Your enemies! Shoot Your arrows and confuse them! Reach down from Heaven and rescue me; rescue me from deep waters, from the power of my enemies.

—Psalm 144:6–7 (NLT)

Indeed, He loves His people; all His holy ones are in His hands.

—Deuteronomy 33:3 (NIV)

Clue: Sing to the tune of, "I Hear Thunder."

Three Wise Friends

Three wise friends.
Three wise friends.

See how they run.
See how they run.

They all sought after the King and prayed,
Lifting me up both night and day.

Have you ever needed help in this way?
Seek three wise friends.

Hidden Treasure

Though one may be overpowered, two can defend themselves. A cord of three strands is not quickly broken.

—Ecclesiastes 4:12 (NIV)

Clue: Sing to the tune of, "Three Blind Mice."

Working for the Kingdom

I'll be working for the kingdom as I live each day.
I'll be working for the kingdom with what I do and say.
Don't you feel the Spirit leading?
Rise up and thank the Lord.
Don't you hear His voice **calling**?
Be like Him more and more.

Hidden Treasure

Whatever you do, work at it with all your heart, as working for the Lord, not for men, since you know that you will receive an inheritance from the Lord as a reward. It is the Lord Christ you are serving.

—Colossians 3:23–24 (NIV)

He must become greater; I must become less.

—John 3:30 (NIV)

Clue: Sing to the tune of, "I've Been working on the Railroad."

I Am His Little Lamb

I am His little lamb, little lamb, little lamb.
I am His little lamb.
He makes me white as snow.

And many places Jesus went, Jesus went, Jesus went,
And many places Jesus went
He asks this lamb to go.

Hidden Treasure

My sheep listen to my voice; I know them, and they follow me.

—John 10:27 (NIV)

"Then the King will say to those on his right, 'Come, you who are blessed by my Father; take your inheritance, the kingdom prepared for you since the creation of the world. For I was hungry and you gave me something to eat, I was thirsty and you gave me something to drink, I was a stranger and you invited me in, I needed clothes and you clothed me, I was sick and you looked after me, I was in prison and you came to visit me.'

—Matthew 25:34–36 (NIV)

Clue: Sing to the tune of, "Mary Had a Little Lamb."

Zac and Will

Zac and Will went up a hill
To get some living water.
Zac came down wearing a crown,
And Will came shortly after.
Joy they got. Home they did trot
As fast as they could scamper.
They went to bed, thankfulness in head,
A hope and a future with God's answer!

Hidden Treasure

"For I know the plans I have for you," says the Lord. "They are plans for good and not disaster, to give you a hope and a future."

—Jeremiah 29:11 (NLT)

Anyone who believes in me may come and drink! For the Scriptures declare, "Rivers of living water will flow from his heart."

—John 7:38 (NLT)

"If you only knew the gift God has for you and who you are speaking to, you would ask me, and I would give you living water."

—John 4:10 (NLT)

Clue: Sing to the tune of, "Jack and Jill."

I'm Soaring

It's raining.
It's pouring.
On eagle's wings I'm soaring.
He lifts my head. "Love you" was said.
His mercies are new every morning.

Hidden Treasure

Those who hope in the Lord will renew their strength. They will soar on wings like eagles; they will run and not grow weary, they will walk and not be faint.

—Isaiah 40:31 (NIV)

Great is his faithfulness; his mercies begin afresh each morning.

—Lamentations 3:23 (NLT)

Jesus replied, "If you only knew the gift God has for you and who you are speaking to, you would ask me, and I would give you living water."

—John 4:10 (NLT)

Clue: Sing to the tune of, "It's Raining, It's Pouring."

Walls, Walls

Jericho, Jericho had tall walls.
Jericho, Jericho, they did fall!
All of her soldiers and all of her men
Could not stop us when God said, "Go in!"

With my God I can scale any wall.
Though I may stumble, I shall not fall.
All the enemy's schemes and all the enemy's plans
Shall never snatch me from His hands!

Hidden Treasure

When the trumpets sounded, the army shouted, and at the sound of the trumpet, when the men gave a loud shout, the wall collapsed; so everyone charged straight in, and they took the city.

—Joshua 6:20 (NIV)

My father, who has given them to me, is greater than all; no one can snatch them out of my Father's hand.

—John 10:29 (NIV)

Clue: Sing to the tune of, "Humpty Dumpty."

Little Miss Mabel

Little Miss Mabel
Sat on a table
To hear what the doctor would say.
Along came the liar,
Who tried to sit by her.
Does he frighten Miss Mabel?
No way!

Hidden Treasure

She is clothed with strength and dignity, and she laughs without fear of the future.

—Proverbs 31:25 (NLT)

But in the coming day no weapon turned against you will succeed. You will silence every voice raised up to accuse you.

—Isaiah 54:17 (NLT)

Clue: Sing to the tune of, "Little Miss Muffet."

Father, Son, and the Holy Spirit

Father, Son, and the Holy Spirit, too
The three are one, it's true.
Whenever I go out,
I will sing about
The Father, Son, and Holy Spirit, too!
Na-na-na-na-na-na-na!

Hidden Treasure

Shout joyful praises to God, all the earth! Sing about the glory of his name! Tell the world how glorious he is.

—Psalm 66:1–2 (NLT)

Clue: Sing to the tune of, "John Jacob Jingleheimer Schmidt."

Father, Father, Quite Amazing

Father, Father, quite amazing.

How do your children **grOW?**
The trials are many, but my grace is plenty,
And joy awaits those who follow.

Hidden Treasure

So be truly glad. There is a wonderful joy ahead, even though you have to endure many trials for a little while.

—1 Peter 1:6 (NLT)

But he said to me, "My grace is sufficient for you, for my power is made perfect in weakness." Therefore I will boast all the more gladly about my weaknesses, so that Christ's power may rest on me.

—2 Corinthians 12:9 (NIV)

Clue: Sing to the tune of, "Mary, Mary, Quite Contrary."

Stomp Your Feet!

Stomp, stomp, stomp your feet.
Crush the enemy.
Mightily, mightily, mightily, mightily
March to victory!

Hidden Treasure

Look, I have given you authority over all the power of the enemy, and you can walk among snakes and scorpions and crush them. Nothing will injure you.

—Luke 10:19 (NLT)

Clue: Sing to the tune of, "Row, Row, Row Your Boat."

Sing Unto the Father

Sing unto the Father.
We are His sons and daughters.
Ashes, ashes
Become beautiful crowns.

Hidden Treasure

To all who mourn in Israel, he will give a crown of beauty for ashes, a joyous blessing instead of mourning, festive praise instead of despair. In their righteousness they will be like great oaks that the Lord has planted for his own glory.

—Isaiah 61:3 (NLT)

The godly trip seven times, but they get up again. But one disaster is enough to overthrow the wicked.

—Proverbs 24:16 (NLT)

Clue: Sing to the tune of, "Ring-a-Ring o' Roses."

What Are His Sons Made of?

What are His sons made of?
What are His sons made of?
Strength and might
armed to fight the good fight:
That's what His sons are made of.

Hidden Treasure

For I can do everything through Christ, who gives me strength.

—Philippians 4:13 (NLT)

I love you, LORD; you are my strength.

—Psalm 18:1 (NLT)

Fight the good fight for the true faith. Hold tightly to the eternal life to which God has called you, which you have confessed so well before many witnesses.

—1 Timothy 6:12 (NLT)

Clue: Sing to the tune of, "What Are Little Boys Made Of."

What Are His Girls Made Of?

What are His girls made of?
What are His girls made of?
Love and humility,
Kindness for all to see:
That's what His girls are made of.

Hidden Treasure

Therefore, as God's chosen people, holy and dearly loved, clothe yourselves with compassion, kindness, humility, gentleness and patience. Bear with each other and forgive whatever grievances you may have against one another. Forgive as the Lord forgave you. And over all these virtues put on love, which binds them all together in perfect unity.

—Colossians 3:12–14 (NIV)

Clue: Sing to the tune of, "What Are Little Girls Made Of."

The Power in His Name

His son prays for a wife. The Father gives a wife.
T-R-U-S-T,
The son gets a wife.
The wife prays for a child. The Father gives a child.
T-R-U-S-T,
The wife gets a child.

They tell about His fame, for they asked in His name.
T-R-U-S-T
The power in His name.

Hidden Treasure

You haven't done this before. Ask, using my name, and you will receive, and you will have abundant joy.

—John 16:24 (NLT)

Trust in the Lord will all your heart, do not depend on your own understanding. Seek his will in all you do and he will show you which path to take.

—Proverbs 3:5–6 (NLT)

Clue: Sing to the tune of, "The Farmer in the Dell."

Branches and Limbs

"Branches and limbs,"
Says the vine we are in.
"You must grow grapes,"
Said the Father who creates.
"When will I produce fruit?"
Says the one with deep roots.
"You will grow strong
As the pruning goes along."
"When will it start?"
Said the fear in my heart.
Here comes the gardener, no need to worry
Here comes the Father pruning for glory.

Hidden Treasure

I am the true grapevine, and my Father is the gardener. He cuts off every branch of mine that doesn't produce fruit, and he prunes the branches that do bear fruit so they will produce even more ... When you produce much fruit, you are my true disciples. This brings great glory to my Father.

—John 15:1–2, 8 (NLT)

Clue: Sing to the tune of, "Oranges and Lemons."

His Gifts for Us

His gifts for us are all around,
all around, all around.
His gifts for us are all around.
Have you seen them lately?
The trees in the field go clap, clap, clap,
clap, clap, clap, clap, clap, clap.
The trees in the field go clap, clap, clap.
Have you seen them lately?

Hidden Treasure

Every good and perfect gift is from above, coming down from the Father of the heavenly lights, who does not change like shifting shadows.

—James 1:17 (NIV)

You will go out in joy and be led forth in peace; the mountains and hills will burst into song before you, and all the trees of the field will clap their hands.

—Isaiah 55:12 (NIV)

Clue: Sing to the tune of, "The Wheels on the Bus."

Mirror, Mirror

Mirror, mirror on the wall,
He has no favorites;
He Loves us all.
Mirror, mirror,
What do you see?
Child of God,
Yep, that's me!

Hidden Treasure

Then Peter began to speak: "I now realize how true it is that God does not show favoritism but accepts men from every nation who fear him and do what is right."

—Acts 10:34–35 (NIV)

For you are all children of God through faith in Jesus Christ.

—Galatians 3:26 (NLT)

Hey, Child So Little

Hey, child so little, be a special utensil.
Reflect the Son who made the moon.
Nothing is impossible for our God.
He is faithful and coming soon!

Hidden Treasure

For nothing is impossible with God.

—Luke 1:37 (NLT)

If you keep yourself pure, you will be a special utensil for honorable use. Your life will be clean, and you will be ready for the Master to use you for every good work.

—2 Timothy 2:21 (NLT)

Clue: Sing to the tune of, "Hey Diddle Diddle."

God, Be Mighty

God, be mighty!
God, be quick!
God, guard me
And keep my night lit!

Hidden Treasure

You light a lamp for me. The Lord, my God, lights up my darkness.

—Psalm 18:28 (NLT)

Come with great power, O God, and rescue me! Defend me with your might. Listen to my prayer, O God. Pay attention to my plea.

—Psalm 54:1–2 (NLT)

The Lord is my light and my salvation so why should I be afraid? The Lord is my fortress, protecting me from danger, so why should I tremble?

—Psalm 27:1 (NLT)

Clue: Sing to the tune of, "Jack Be Nimble."

This Little Prince and Princess

This little prince
Works for the department.

This little princess
Works at home.

This little prince
Raises choice beef.

This little princess
Wonders, "What shall I become?"

Hidden Treasure

So whether you eat or drink, or whatever you do, do it all for the glory of God.

—1 Corinthians 10:31 (NLT)

Work with enthusiasm, as though you were working for the Lord rather than for people.

—Ephesians 6:7 (NLT)

Clue: Sing to the tune of, "This Little Piggy."

One, Two, God Loves You!

One, two, God loves you.
Three, four, He opens doors.
Five, six, beware of tricks.
Seven, eight, go through the narrow gate.

Nine, ten, with **JESUS we WIN**!

Hidden Treasure

For the Father Himself loves you dearly because you love me and believe that I came from God.

—John 16:27 (NLT)

And so I tell you, keep on asking, and you will receive what you ask for. Keep on seeking, you will find. Keep on knocking, and the door will be opened to you.

—Luke 11:9 (NLT)

Then we will no longer be immature like children. We won't be tossed and blown about by every wind of new teaching. We will not be influenced when people try to trick us with lies so clever they sound like the truth.

—Ephesians 4:14 (NLT)

You can enter God's kingdom only through the narrow gate. The highway to hell is broad, and its gate is wide for the many who choose that way.

—Matthew 7:13 (NLT)

And who can win this battle against the world? Only those who believe that Jesus is the Son of God.

—1 John 5:5 (NLT)

Clue: Sing to the tune of, "One Two Buckle My Shoe."

He Loves Me

He loves me.
He loves me a lot.
He loves me.
He loves me a lot.
Fail me? No, He will not!
I love the Lord.
I love Him a lot.
Forget him? No, I will not!

Hidden Treasure

For the Father himself loves you dearly because you love me and believe that I came from God.

—John 16:27 (NLT)

I love you, O Lord, my strength.

—Psalm 18:1 (NIV)

When the Lord your God brings you into the land he swore to your fathers, to Abraham, Isaac, and Jacob, to give you a land with large, flourishing cities you did not build, houses filled with all kinds of good things you did not provide, wells you did not dig, and vineyards and olive groves you did not plant then when you eat and are satisfied, be careful that you do not forget the Lord, who brought you out of Egypt, out of the land of slavery.

—Deuteronomy 6:10–12 (NIV)

One Disciple, Two Disciples

One disciple,
Two disciples,
Three disciples—
Wow, now four!
Five disciples,
Six disciples,
Seven disciples—
Go make more!

Hidden Treasure

Therefore, go and make disciples of all the nations, baptizing them in the name of the Father and the Son and the Holy Spirit. Teach these new disciples to obey all commands I have given you. And be sure of this: I am with you always, even to the end of the age.

—Matthew 28:19–20 (NLT)

Clue: Sing to the tune of, "One Potato, Two Potato."

There Is a Father Who Lives in Heaven

Our Father lives in Heaven,
It's true!
He has so many kids
He knows exactly what to do!
He will give them today
Their daily bread,
And they can sleep safely
When they go off to bed.

Hidden Treasure

This, then, is how you should pray: "Our Father in heaven, hallowed be your name, your kingdom come, your will be done on earth as it is in heaven. Give us today our daily bread. Forgive our debts, as we also have forgiven our debtor. And lead us not into temptation but deliver us from the evil one."
—Matthew 6:9–13 (NIV)

I will lie down and sleep in peace, for you alone, O Lord, make me dwell in safety.
—Psalm 4:8 (NIV)

Clue: Sing to the tune of, "There was an Old Woman Who Lived in a Shoe."

Prodigal, Prodigal the Father's Son

Prodigal, prodigal, the Father's son,
Feeding the pigs, for he chose to run.
The son was beat and longed to eat,
And the Father went running down to greet!

Hidden Treasure

Jesus continued: "There was a man who had two sons. The younger one said to his father, 'Father, give me my share of the estate,' So he divided his property between them. Not long after that, the younger son got together all he had, set off for a distant country and there squandered his wealth in wild living. After he had spent everything, there was a severe famine in that whole country, and he began to be in need. So he went and hired himself out to a citizen of that country, who sent him to his fields to feed pigs. He longed to fill his stomach with the pods that the pigs were eating, but no one gave him anything. When he came to his senses, he said, 'How many of my father's hired men have food to spare, and here I am starving to death! I will set out and go back to my father and say to him: Father I have sinned against heaven and against you. I am no longer worthy to be called you son; make me like one of your hired men.' So he got up and went to his father. But while he was still a long way off, his father saw him and was filled with compassion for him; he ran to his son, threw his arms around him and kissed him."

—Luke 15:11–20 (NIV)

Clue: Sing to the tune of, "Tom, Tom, the Piper's Son."

Our Heavenly Father

Our heavenly Father
Has a Son,
And Jesus is His name-**O**!
J-E-S-U-S, J-E-S-U-S, J-E-S-U-S!
What power is in His name-**O**!

Hidden Treasure

But I will reveal my name to my people, and they will come to know its power. Then at last they will recognize that I am the one who speaks to them.

—Isaiah 52:6 (NLT)

Clue: Sing to the tune of, "Bingo/Bingo Was His Name-O."

Who?

Who do we belong to?
The King of Kings;
He is faithful and true.
Whose voice can we hear?
Wonderful Counselor
Will draw us near.
Whose hand holds us tight?
Abba, Father,
Day and night.
Whose blood justifies us?
Jesus Christ:
In him we trust!

Hidden Treasure

On his robe and on his thigh was written this title: King of kings and Lord of lords.

—Revelation 19:16 (NLT)

My Father, who has given them to me, is greater than all; no one can snatch them out of my Father's hand.

—John 10:29 (NIV)

But God demonstrates his own love for us in this: While we were still sinners, Christ died for us. Since we have now been justified by his blood, how much more shall we be saved from God's wrath through him!

—Romans 5:8–9 (NIV)

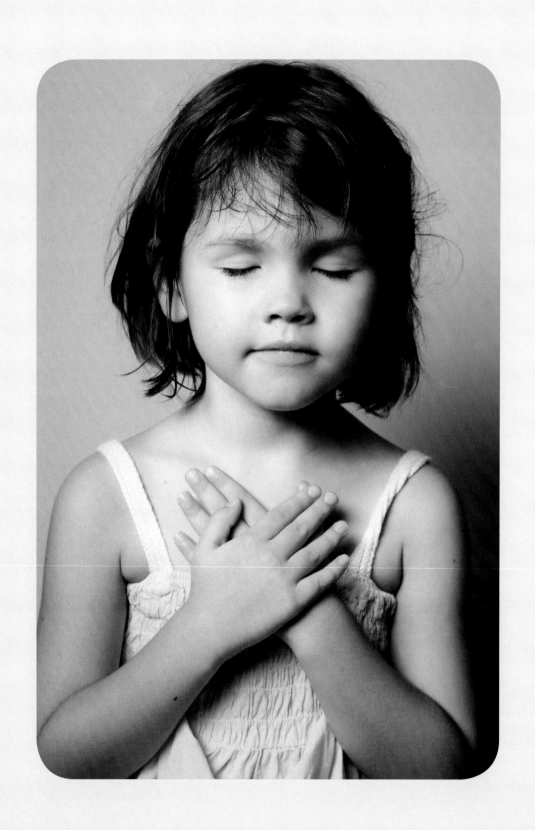

Providing Love

A-tisket a-tasket,
Leftovers filled twelve baskets!
This act showed His providing love.
Be on your way; go feed some.
Go feed some. Go feed some.
Be on your way; go feed some.
Help little ones eat it up,
Store in their hearts and lock it up.

Hidden Treasure

But Jesus said, "You feed them." "But we have only five loaves of bread and two fish," they answered. "Or are you expecting us to go and buy enough food for this whole crowd?" For there were about 5,000 men there. Jesus replied, "Tell them to sit down in groups of about fifty each." So the people all sat down. Jesus took the five loaves and two fish, looked up toward heaven, and blessed them. Then, breaking the loaves into pieces, he kept giving the bread and fish to the disciples so they could distribute it to the people. They all ate as much as they wanted, and afterward, the disciples picked up twelve baskets of leftovers!

—Luke 9:13–17 (NLT)

But Jesus told him, "No! The Scriptures say, 'People do not live by bread alone, but by every word that comes from the mouth of God.'"

—Matthew 4:4 (NLT)

"Listen to his instructions, and store them in your heart ... I have not departed from his commands, but have treasured his words more than daily food."

—Job 22:22, 23:12 (NLT)

Clue: Sing to the tune of, "A-Tisket A-Tasket."

Wretched Man Again

Here comes that wretched man in me again.
He's shouting, "No, you don't have to forgive again!"
Along comes the Spirit and whispers, "Yes, again!"
Poor old wretched man in me again!
Try again!
Forgive again!

Hidden Treasure

I know that nothing good lives in me, that is, in my sinful nature. For I have the desire to do what is good, but I cannot carry it out … What a wretched man I am! Who will rescue me from this body of death? Thanks be to God through Jesus Christ our Lord!"

—Romans 7:18, 24–25 (NIV)

"Then Peter came to Jesus and asked, "Lord, how many times shall I forgive my brother when he sins against me? Up to seven times?" Jesus answered, "I tell you, not seven times, but seventy-seven times."

—Matthew 18:21–22 (NIV)

Clue: Sing to the tune of, "There Was an Old Man Called Michael Finnegan."

I'm a Little Clay Pot

I'm a little clay pot, cracked yet stout,
Made by God and loved no doubt.
When He shines on me, His Spirit blooms out.
Go ahead and pick fruit out!

Hidden Treasure

And yet, O Lord, you are our Father. We are the clay, and you are the potter. We all are formed by your hand."

—Isaiah 64:8 (NLT)

But we have this treasure in jars of clay to show that this all-surpassing power is from God and not from us.

—2 Corinthians 4:7 (NIV)

But the fruit of the Spirit is love, joy, peace, patience, kindness, goodness, faithfulness, gentleness, and self-control. Against such things there is no law.

—Galatians 5:22-23 (NIV)

Clue: Sing to the tune of, "I'm a Little Tea Pot."

The Seed

One, two, three, four, five
Protect the seed—it is alive.
Six, seven, eight, nine, ten
Here come those pesky birds again.
Why won't I let it go?
Because it is meant to grow.
When will they take flight?

As I **stand** in **faith** and **might**.

Hidden Treasure

This is the meaning of the parable: The seed is the word of God. Those along the path are the ones who hear, and then the devil comes and takes away the word from their hearts, so that they may not believe and be saved. Those on the rock are the ones who receive the word with joy when they hear it, but they have no root. They believe for a while, but in the time of testing they fall away. The seed that fell among thorns stands for those who hear, but as they go on their way they are choked by life's worries, riches and pleasures, and they do not mature. But the seed on good soil stands for those with a noble and good heart, who hear the word, retain it, and by persevering produce a crop.

—Luke 8:11–15 (NIV)

Stand firm against him, and be strong in your faith. Remember that your Christian brothers and sisters all over the world are going through the same kind of suffering you are.

—1 Peter 5:9 (NLT)

Clue: Sing to the tune of, "One, Two, Three, Four, Five."

Thoughts

One thought,
Two thoughts,
Three thoughts,
Four:
They are so many,
Outnumbering the sand along His shores.

Hidden Treasure

How precious are your thoughts about me, O God. They cannot be numbered! I can't even count them; they outnumber the grains of sand! And when I wake up, you are still with me!

—Psalm 139: 17–18 (NLT)

Clue: Sing to the tune of, "One Potato, Two Potato."

Oh, My Sweet Baby

Oh, my sweet baby, go to the top.
When the storm blows, hide in the Rock.
Though the earth quakes and mountains may fall,
Up will He hold you,
Shielding through all.

Hidden Treasure

The Lord is my rock, my fortress, and my savior; my God is my rock, in whom I find protection.
He is my shield, the power that saves me, and my place of safety.

—Psalm 18:2 (NLT)

God is our refuge and strength, an ever-present help in trouble. Therefore we will not fear, though
the earth give way and the mountains fall into the heart of the sea, though its waters roar and foam
and the mountains quake with their surging.

—Psalm 46:2 (NIV)

Clue: Sing to the tune of, "Rock-a-Bye, Baby."

Childlike Faith

Childlike faith,
Childlike faith:
The kingdom awaits those
With childlike faith.

Hidden Treasure

But Jesus called the children to him and said, "Let the little children come to me, and do not hinder them, for the kingdom of God belongs to such as these. I tell you the truth, anyone who will not receive the kingdom of God like a little child will never enter it."

—Luke 18:16–17 (NIV)

Four-Leaf Clovers

Four-leaf clovers
Are such a rare find,
Not bringing luck,
But they do bring to mind:
I'm created by God,
His very unique design!

Hidden Treasure

I praise you because I am fearfully and wonderfully made; your works are wonderful, I know that full well.

—Psalm 139:14 (NIV)

Find a Penny

Find a penny,
Pick it up.
Thank God
For the blessing I've struck!
Whether it is heads or tails
Makes no difference,
He will not fail.
Superstition—not for me.
Thankful for the penny I see,
For when I pick it up,
I will thank Him for His favor, not luck.
He sees and watches all,
Even knows when sparrows fall.
The hairs on my head, He has the number.
Did you know He never slumbers?
What an awesome God we serve!
Go ahead and spread the Word!

Hidden Treasure

Are not two sparrows sold for a penny? Yet not one of them will fall to the ground apart from the will of your Father. And even the very hairs of your head are all numbered. So don't be afraid; you are worth more than many sparrows.

—Matthew 10:29–31 (NIV)

From heaven the Lord looks down and sees all mankind; from his dwelling place he watches all who live on earth---he who forms the heart of all, who considers everything they do.

—Psalm 33:13-15 (NIV)

Blow and Pray

Blow and pray
Thanksgiving in
Whatever comes your way.
As they fly in the air,
Trust and remember
How deeply he cares.

Hidden Treasure

Because he bends down to listen, I will pray as long as I have breath!

—Psalm 116:2 (NLT)

Do not be anxious about anything, but in everything, by prayer and petition, with thanksgiving present your request to God. And the peace of God which transcends all understanding, will guard your hearts and minds in Christ Jesus.

—Philippians 4:6–7 (NIV)

Give all your worries and cares to God, for he cares about you.

—1 Peter 5:7 (NLT)

Today Is the Day

Today is the day I seek the Lord,
Seek the Lord, seek the Lord.
Today is the day I seek the Lord
So early in the morning.
Today is the day I rejoice in Him,
Rejoice in Him, rejoice in Him.
Today is the day I rejoice in Him
So early in the morning.

Hidden Treasure

Listen to my voice in the morning, LORD. Each morning I bring my requests to you and wait expectantly.

—Psalm 5:3 (NLT)

Rejoice in the Lord always. I will say it again: Rejoice! Let your gentleness be evident to all. The Lord is near. Do not be anxious about anything, but in everything by prayer and petition, with thanksgiving, present your request to God. And the peace of God, which transcends all understanding will guard your hearts and minds in Christ Jesus.

—Philippians 4:4–7 (NIV)

Clue: Sing to the tune of, "This is the Way."

Hallelujah

Hallelujah, praise Him always
My oh my, it's a glorious day
Plenty of blessings heading my way
Hallelujah, praise Him always
I am safe between His shoulders
He's the Truth, the Savior
Never will I fear in danger

Hidden Treasure

I will extol the LORD at all times; His praise will always be on my lips.

—Psalm 34:1 (NIV)

Praise the LORD. How good it is to sing praises to our God, how pleasant and fitting to praise him!

—Psalm 147:1 (NIV)

About Benjamin he said: "Let the beloved of the Lord rest secure in him, for he shields him all day long, and the one the Lord loves rests between his shoulders."

—Deuteronomy 33:12 (NIV)

Clue: Sing to the tune of, "Zip-A-Dee-Doo-Dah."

you Are My Son-shine

You are my Son-shine, my only Son-shine
You make me hopeful when life is grey
I'll never know, Lord, how much you love me
And you'll never take it away
You go before me, you are behind me
I am held fast in all my days
I'll never know, Lord, how much you love me
And you'll never take it away

Hidden Treasure

Jesus spoke to the people once more and said, "I am the light of the world. If you follow me, you won't have to walk in darkness, because you will have the light that leads to life."

—John 8:12 (NLT)

The Lord delights in those who fear him, who put their hope in his unfailing love.

—Psalm 147:11 (NIV)

The Lord himself goes before you and will be with you; he will never leave you nor forsake you. Do not be afraid; do not be discouraged.

—Deuteronomy 31:8 (NIV)

Clue: Sing to the tune of, "You Are My Sunshine."

When you Seek the Morning Star

When you seek the Morning Star,
Makes no difference where you are.
He loves to hear your heart's desire;
He cares for you.
Delight in him and dream a dream.
No request is too extreme
When you seek the Morning Star
As children do.

Hidden Treasure

Now to him who is able to do immeasurably more than all we ask or imagine, according to his power that is at work within us, to him be all glory in the church and in Christ Jesus throughout all generations, for ever and ever! Amen.

—Ephesians 3:20-21(NIV)

O Lord, what is man that you care for him, the son of man that you think of him?

—Psalm 144:3 (NIV)

Delight yourself in the Lord, and he will give you the desires of your heart.

—Psalm 37:4 (ESV)

"I Jesus, have sent my angel to give you this testimony for the churches. I am the Root and the Offspring of David, and the bright Morning Star."

Clue: Sing to the tunes of, "When You Wish Upon a Star."

My Child Walks

My child walks like this and that.
She is not too tall and never too fat.
I've given her fingers;
I've given her toes,
And please do not criticize
Her perfectly shaped nose.

Hidden Treasure

All beautiful you are, my darling; there is no flaw in you.

—Song of Songs 4:7 (NIV)

With his mouth the godless man would destroy his neighbor, but by knowledge the righteous are delivered.

—Proverbs 11:9 (ESV)

May the words of my mouth and the meditation of my heart be pleasing to you, O LORD, my rock and my redeemer.

—Psalm 19:14 (NLT)

Clue: Sing to the tune of, "An Elephant Walks."

Baa, Baa, My Sheep

Baa, baa my sheep,
Have you any tools?
Yes Lord, yes Lord
My heart is full.
Scripture for comfort.
Scripture to obey
At times speaking loudly,
Lighting up my way.

My son, pay attention to what I say; listen closely to my words. Do not let them out of your sight, keep them within your heart, for they are life to those who find them and health to a man's whole body. Above all else, guard your heart, for it is the wellspring of life. Put away perversity from your mouth; keep corrupt talk far from your lips. Let your eyes look straight ahead, fix your gaze directly before you.

—Proverbs 4:20-25 (NIV)

I have hidden your word in my heart, that I might not sin against you.

—Psalm 119:11 (NLT)

Your word is a lamp to guide my feet and a light for my path.

—Psalm119:105 (NLT)

Clue: Sing to the tune of, "Baa, Baa Black Sheep"

One Beautiful, Hopeful Morning

One beautiful, hopeful morning,
All though darkness black as night,
There I met my savior,
Saved by his might.
He began to shelter
And I began to see
I am with you
As You sang over me.

Hidden Treasure

The Lord your God is with you, he is mighty to save. He will take great delight in you, he will quiet you with his love, he will rejoice over you with singing.

—Zephaniah 3:17 (NIV)

Clue: Sing to the tune of, "One Misty, Moisty Morning."

Rain, Rain, Come Today

Rain, rain, come today,
Showering blessings along my way,
Trusting you'll do as you say.

Hidden Treasure

"Bring the whole tithe into the storehouse. Test me in this," says the Lord Almighty, "and see if I will not open the floodgates of heaven and pour out so much blessing that you will not have room enough for it."

—Malachi 3:10 (NIV)

Clue: Sing to the tune of, "Rain, Rain, Go Away."

I'm Praising in the Rain

I'm praising in the rain
Just, praising in the rain
What a peaceful feeling
I'm held once again
I'm singing in the pain
Just, singing in the pain
What a awesome feeling
My eyes are on Him.

Hidden Treasure

I will praise you as long as I live, and in your name I will lift up my hands. My soul will be satisfied as with the richest of foods; with singing lips my mouth will praise you. On my bed I remember you; I think of you through the watches of the night. Because you are my help, I sing in the shadow of your wings. My soul clings to you; your right hand upholds me.

—Psalm63:4-8 (NIV)

The LORD hears his people when they call for help. He rescues them from all their troubles. The LORD is close to the brokenhearted; he rescues those whose spirits are crushed.

—Psalm 34:17-18 (NLT)

We do this by keeping our eyes on Jesus, the champion who initiates and perfects our faith. Because of the joy awaiting him, he endured the cross, disregarding its shame. Now he is seated in the place of honor beside God's throne.

—Hebrews 12: 2 (NLT)

Clue: Sing to the tune of, "Singin' in the Rain."

Sing a Song of Hope

Sing, sing a song.
Make it hopeful.
Help others sing along.
Don't think that you're not good enough!
The Father loves to hear.
You sing,
Sing a song!

Hidden Treasure

Find rest, O my soul, in God alone; my hope comes from him.

—Psalm 62:5 (NIV)

Because you are my help, I will sing in the shadow of your wings.

—Psalm 63:7 (NIV)

Clue: Sing to the tune of, "Sing"

Father, Father, Here's My Heart

Father, Father, here's my heart.
I am ready for you to start.
My repenting is never too late.
Coming through you my trustworthy gate.
Father, Father, here's my heart
I am ready for you to start

Hidden Treasure

And I will give you a new heart, and I will put a new spirit in you. I will take out your stony, stubborn heart and give you a tender, responsive heart. And I will put my Spirit in you so that you will follow my decrees and be careful to obey my regulations.

—Ezekiel 36:26 (NLT)

In the same way, there is more joy in heaven over one lost sinner who repents and returns to God than over ninety-nine others who are righteous and haven't strayed away!

—Luke 15:7 (NLT)

Those who heard Jesus use this illustration didn't understand what he meant, so he explained it to them: "I tell you the truth, I am the gate for the sheep. All who came before me were thieves and robbers. Yes, I am the gate. Those who come in through me will be saved. They will come and go freely and will find good pasture. The thief's purpose is to steal and kill and destroy. My purpose is to give them a rich and satisfying life."

—John 10:6-10 (NLT)

Clue: Sing to the tune of, "Cobbler, Cobbler, Mend My Shoe."

Little Child Fully Dressed

Little child fully dressed
The Father sees thee
The enemy laid his trap but wisdom said flee
Crushed was his tricky plan, and away he ran
Says little child fully dressed,
"In Christ Power I praise and stand!"
Little child told about his deliverance that day
With my Jesus
There is always a way

Hidden Treasure

Finally, be strong in the Lord and in his mighty power. Put on the full armor of God so that you can take your stand against the devil's schemes.

—Ephesians 10:10-11 (NIV)

No temptation has seized you except what is common to man. And God is faithful; he will not let you be tempted beyond what you can bear. But when you are tempted, he will also provide a way out so that you can stand up under it.

—1 Corinthians 10:13 (NIV)

Come and listen to me, all you who fear God; let me tell you what he has done for me. I cried out to him with my mouth; his praise was on my tongue.

—Psalm 66:16-17 (NIV

Clue: Sing to the tune of, "Little Robin Redbreast."

Feet and Toes

Eeny, meeny, miney, mo,
Thank God for your feet and toes.

With a shout and trumpet blow
In the clouds we'll meet and go.

Eeny, meeny, miney, mo,
Thank God for your feet and toes.

Hidden Treasure

For the Lord himself will come down from heaven, with a loud command, with the voice of the archangel and with the trumpet call of God, and the dead in Christ will rise first. After that, we who are still alive and are left will be caught up together with them in the clouds to meet the Lord in the air. And so we will be with the Lord forever. Therefore encourage each other with these words.

—1Thessalonians 4:16-18 (NIV)

Clue: Sing to the tune of, "Eeny, Meeny."

White Horse

White horse, white horse, don't you stop,
Bring our Savior come clippety clop;
His sword goes swish,
The enemy goes down;
Giddy-up, we are victory bound!

Hidden Treasure

Then I saw heaven opened, and a white horse was standing there. Its rider was named Faithful and True, for he judges fairly and wages a righteous war.

—Revelations 19:11 (NLT)

All who are victorious will inherit these blessings, and I will be their God, and they will be my children.

—Revelations 21:7 (NLT)

Clue: Sing to the tune of, "Horsie, Horsie."

Throw a Net, Throw a Net

Throw a net, throw a net, fisherman,
Catch as many people as you can.

Tell them they are loved.
Baptize in my name.
A home now awaits and forever they will stay!

Hidden Treasure

Jesus called out to them, "Come, follow me, and I will show you how to fish for people!"
—Mathew 4:19 (NLT)

Peter replied, "Each of you must repent of your sins and turn to God, and be baptized in the name of Jesus Christ for the forgiveness of your sins. Then you will receive the gift of the Holy Spirit.
—Acts 2:38 (NLT)

Clue: Sing to the tune of, "Pat-a-cake, Pat-a-cake."

Shine light, shine bright.

Shine light, shine bright,
Bend down to me tonight,
I pray I may, I pray I might ,
Have the prayer I prayed tonight.

Hidden Treasure:

When Jesus spoke again to the people, he said," I am the light of the world. Whoever follows me will never walk in darkness, but will have the light of life.

—John 8:12 (NIV)

Because he bends down to listen, I will pray as long as I have breath!

—Psalm 116:2 (NLT)

Child of God,

The LORD bless you and keep you; the LORD make his face **shine** upon you and be gracious to you; the LORD turn his face toward you and give you peace.

Blessings,
Shelley Vieira

If you would like to begin a personal relationship with Jesus today,
please pray this prayer:

Lord Jesus, I invite You into my life,
I believe You died for me and that your blood pays
for my sins and provides me with the gift of eternal life;
By faith I receive that gift and thank you for the Holy
Spirit that will now help me in this life.
I accept You as my Lord and Savior. Amen.